Under the Helmet

Stephen 'Spitty' Spiteri

Front cover photo credit: Cameron Drendel (@_bittermedia)

Rear cover photo credit: Sam Mule (@perth_yammy)

Cover design by Ven Visual (@venvisualau)

Interior design by Red Feather Publishing (@redfeatherpublishing)

ISBN: Print 9781764576208

ISBN: E-book 978176457615

CONTENTS

DEDICATION

To my wife, S—

My wife of twenty years... and still counting.

For your steady support of everything I have ever attempted, and for your honesty when something truly was a bad idea. You have always been my anchor, my voice of reason, and the person who kept me grounded when enthusiasm needed tempering. I would not have had the freedom to pursue anything meaningful without the stability you provided. You have always been my rock.

To my children, R, E, and M—

For seeing me as Superman, even when I have been far from it. For loving me through my lowest moments without condition or calculation. You reminded me, often without knowing it, of the sheer privilege of being your dad.

Mum and Dad—

For the values you lived more than you taught. For showing me what consistency, responsibility, and quiet effort look like over time.

Much of what holds me steady began with you.

To the Perth (Western Australia) motorcycle community—

For the welcome I didn't have to earn, and the inclusiveness I didn't expect.

For the people doing amazing things, riding well, and setting standards without needing attention.

And for the shared lanes, shared coffees, and the rides that reminded me I wasn't doing this alone.

Author's Note

I did not write this book as an expert.

I wrote it as someone who spent a long time functioning well enough while quietly carrying more than was necessary. Like many men, I learned early how to endure. I learned how to be useful, reliable, and composed. I learned how to keep moving. What I did not learn—at least not until later—was how to regulate my attention, my limits, and my internal load with the same seriousness I applied to everything else.

Motorcycle riding entered my life at a point when I was not broken, but I was not settled either. Riding did not save me. It did not fix anything. What it did was reveal something I had lost touch with: the stabilising effect of responsibility made concrete. Attention demanded rather than requested. Consequence made visible. Maintenance rendered non-negotiable.

That experience sent me back to questions I had been circling for years—about masculinity, discipline, risk, mental health, and what it actually means to live well under load. Philosophy gave language to what riding made tangible. Counselling gave structure to what regulation alone could not resolve. None of it was dramatic. All of it mattered.

This book is not a manifesto, a self-help program, or a romanticisation of motorcycles. It is a series of reflections on attention, responsibility, and maintenance—examined through riding, but intended for life off the bike. It does not argue that men should ride motorcycles. It argues that men need practices that impose order rather than promise comfort.

If you are looking for motivation, this book will likely disappoint you. If you are looking for permission to avoid difficult conversations or inner work, it will disappoint you even more. What it offers instead is clarity: quiet, practical, and occasionally uncomfortable.

Everything here is written from experience rather than theory alone. What resonated for me may not resonate for you in exactly the same way. That is fine. The aim is not agreement. It is usefulness.

Read this book slowly or in one sitting. Highlight nothing if you like. Argue with it if you need to. Take what holds and leave what doesn't. But if it prompts you to take your attention, your limits, and your maintenance a little more seriously, it has done its work.

The helmet goes on. The visor drops. The ride begins.

What matters most is what you bring back with you.

Memento Mori

Memento Vivere

Introduction

Under the Helmet

"You have power over your mind — not outside events. Realise this, and you will find strength."

— *Marcus Aurelius*

There is a moment before every ride when the world contracts.

The helmet goes on. The visor drops. The sound changes. Not to silence—but to something manageable. Breathing gets louder. The noise that matters stays. The rest falls away.

You are no longer reacting. You are participating.

For a lot of men, that moment isn't about speed or rebellion. It's about order.

This book begins there.

For some men, motorcycles have become one of the few places where the mind settles rather than scatters. Not because riding is escapism, but because it demands something modern life rarely does: full presence. Riding doesn't allow partial attention. It doesn't tolerate rumination. It rewards discipline and punishes carelessness. Thought, action, and consequence are forced into alignment.

That alignment is stabilising.

This isn't an argument that motorcycles are therapy. They're not. Riding won't cure anxiety, depression, or the quiet dissatisfaction many men carry around without a name. Anyone who claims otherwise is selling a fantasy. But riding *can* regulate the mind. It can interrupt spirals. It can create enough space for clarity to return.

Under the helmet, many men experience a calm that feels earned rather than manufactured. Not numbness. Not distraction. A steady attentiveness rooted in responsibility. Throttle. Clutch. Brake. Line. Input followed by consequence. Immediate, honest feedback. No room for self-deception.

This is why riding resonates with men who value competence.

There's also a particular kind of solitude involved. Riding solitude isn't isolation. It's engagement without audience. No performance. No explaining yourself. Just judgement, risk management, and presence. For men who spend most of their lives being useful, accountable, and available to others—at work, at home, in family—that kind of solitude restores rather than indulges.

But this book is just as concerned with restraint.

The same focus that calms the mind can become avoidance if it's misused. Riding can regulate emotion—or suppress it. It can sharpen awareness—or delay conversations that need to happen. Philosophy demands honesty here. If riding becomes the only place you feel ordered, something else is being neglected.

Mental health isn't about feeling good. It's about functioning well. It's maintenance, not motivation. Strong men don't ignore this work; they approach it with the same seriousness they bring to their machines. Maintenance is masculine. Neglect isn't.

What follows is a series of reflections on attention, risk, responsibility, and masculinity—viewed through the lens of riding, but not confined to it. It argues for discipline over recklessness, competence over bravado, and responsibility as the foundation of freedom. These ideas aren't fashionable, but they endure.

Under the helmet there's no applause and no metrics. Just presence. That simplicity isn't an escape from life; it's a reminder of how life works when it's stripped back to essentials.

Every ride ends. The helmet comes off. Whatever was waiting before the ride is still there.

The question is whether you return more capable of meeting it.

1

NOT BROKEN, BUT NOT FINE

"No man is crushed by misfortune unless he has first been deceived by prosperity."

— Seneca

For a long time, I didn't think of myself as someone with "mental health issues."

I was functioning. That's the word we use. Functioning.

I was working. I was present for my family. I paid the bills, met my obligations, and showed up when required. Nothing was visibly falling apart. From the outside, everything looked fine—and in many ways, it was.

But functioning isn't the same thing as being well.

There's a psychological state a lot of men live in where nothing is bad enough to justify intervention, yet nothing is settled enough to feel steady. You're not broken. But you're not fine either. You carry a low-level tension that never quite resolves. It hums in the background—quiet, manageable, constant, and tiring.

This isn't crisis. It's attrition.

I wasn't waking up anxious in the clinical sense. I wasn't having panic attacks or dramatic emotional swings. What I experienced instead was compression: responsibility, expectation, noise, and internal pressure stacking up without release. Each demand made sense on its own. Together, they created a mental load that never fully switched off.

Men are good at enduring this.

We mistake endurance for health. We interpret tolerance as strength. As long as we're not failing publicly, we assume things are acceptable. We adapt. We compartmentalise. We get on with it. And because the system keeps running, we convince ourselves it must be working.

But systems can function while they're degrading.

Over time, I noticed small changes. My attention fractured more easily. Silence became uncomfortable. Rest stopped restoring me. Even when things were calm, my mind was scanning, planning, anticipating. My body was present. My attention wasn't.

That kind of state is hard to describe, especially for men used to solving problems rather than naming them. There's no obvious enemy. No single cause to remove. Just a sense that something is slightly out of alignment and getting heavier to carry.

Philosophically, it's an order problem.

Human beings function best when thought, action, and responsibility line up. When they drift—when you think one thing, do another, and feel pulled in conflicting directions—tension accumulates. Not enough to break you. Enough to wear you down.

I didn't recognise this as a mental health issue at first because it didn't match the stories I'd absorbed. Mental health, as it's usually presented, looks dramatic or clinical. What I was experiencing felt ordinary. Mundane. Almost boring. And yet it persisted.

The danger is that it becomes normal.

When low-level stress becomes your baseline, you forget what steadiness feels like. You adjust expectations downward. You accept a diminished version of yourself as the cost of responsibility. And because you're still functioning, you rarely feel entitled to question it.

This is where a lot of men stop reflecting and start enduring.

Nothing dramatic changed things for me. There was no breakdown. No intervention. Just a gradual realisation that my internal state didn't match the life I was working to maintain. I was doing everything "right," yet something essential felt perpetually unresolved.

The question arrived quietly: *If this is sustainable, why does it feel so heavy?*

That question matters. It shifts the frame from weakness to alignment. It doesn't ask whether you *can* endure something. It asks whether you *should*.

Mental health, in this sense, isn't about eliminating discomfort. It's about whether your internal resources are keeping pace with your external demands. When they don't, something gives. Usually attention, patience, or presence.

I didn't want to become someone permanently braced against life.

That's where the idea of maintenance started to matter.

2

LEARNING TO LIVE WITH NOISE

"If you seek tranquility, do less — but do what is essential."

— *Marcus Aurelius*

The difficulty with mental noise is not that it is loud.

It is that it is constant.

Noise, in this sense, is not chaos or crisis. It is accumulation. It is the steady layering of unfinished thoughts, low-level vigilance, and unspoken responsibility. It is the mental equivalent of leaving too many tabs open at once—not enough to crash the system, but enough to slow everything down.

For a long time, I thought this was simply adulthood.

You carry work in your head after hours. You replay conversations. You anticipate problems before they arrive. You plan contingencies. You stay one step ahead because that's what being responsible looks like. None of this feels pathological. In fact, much of it is rewarded.

The trouble is that the mind doesn't know when to stand down.

What begins as preparedness becomes background tension. What begins as care becomes constant monitoring. The internal commentary never quite stops, even when nothing urgent is happening. The body rests, but the mind remains braced.

I didn't experience this as anxiety in the obvious sense. There were no racing heartbeats or moments of panic. What I experienced was a kind of mental compression—a narrowing of internal space. Thoughts overlapped. Silence filled itself automatically. Even downtime carried a faint edge of restlessness, as though I should be doing something else.

And because this state was manageable, I normalised it.

That's the danger.

When mental noise becomes the baseline, you stop noticing it as noise. It becomes the water you're swimming in. You adapt. You compensate. You function. And because you are still meeting your obligations, you assume nothing is wrong.

But something is happening.

Attention becomes fragmented. Patience shortens slightly. Curiosity dulls. Rest stops restoring. You might still enjoy things, but enjoyment feels thinner. Less spacious. The mind is always half elsewhere, scanning ahead, bracing for what's next.

This is not burnout. It's earlier than that.

It's the stage where endurance replaces regulation.

I was good at enduring.

Like many men, I had learned to tolerate internal strain without naming it. I didn't complain. I didn't collapse. I didn't feel justified in asking for help. I simply carried on, assuming this was the cost of being useful, reliable, and responsible.

Philosophically, this is where things start to drift.

The Stoics warned against allowing the mind to be governed by what it does not control. Modern life does the opposite. It trains us to attend to everything simultaneously—emails, deadlines, expectations, hypothetical futures—many of which we can influence only marginally, if at all.

The result is a mind that is busy but rarely settled.

I noticed that silence had become uncomfortable.

Not threatening—just crowded. In quiet moments, thoughts rushed in to fill the space. Tasks replayed. Conversations looped. Hypotheticals multiplied. Even leisure came with a sense of inefficiency, as though time not actively producing something was being wasted.

This isn't a character flaw. It's a predictable outcome.

The modern environment is noisy by design. It fragments attention, rewards urgency, and rarely signals completion. There is always something left unfinished. Something that could be improved. Something waiting for a response. Without deliberate boundaries, that noise migrates inward.

At first, I tried to manage it cognitively.

I prioritised. I organised. I rationalised. I told myself this was simply what a full life felt like. That everyone lived this way. That competence required constant engagement. These explanations weren't wrong—but they were incomplete.

They explained why the noise existed, not why it felt increasingly corrosive.

The problem wasn't effort. It was lack of closure.

Attention, when continuously divided, becomes fatigued. Fatigued attention seeks relief. Often, that relief comes through distraction—scrolling, snacking, numbing, anything that interrupts the pressure briefly. But distraction doesn't resolve noise. It postpones it.

What I hadn't learned was how to interrupt noise deliberately.

Endurance had become my default strategy. If things felt heavy, I carried more carefully. If my mind felt crowded, I pushed through. If rest didn't work, I assumed I needed better discipline.

What I didn't question was whether the system itself needed regulation.

Living with noise is possible. Many men do it for decades. But over time, noise reshapes you. It makes you more reactive. Less patient. Less present. Not because you choose to be that way, but because your cognitive resources are constantly being consumed.

This matters ethically, not just personally.

A man who is perpetually mentally occupied has less to give. Less attention for the people in front of him. Less patience for ambiguity. Less clarity when making decisions that affect others. Noise doesn't stay contained—it leaks outward.

I didn't want to become someone who was physically present but mentally elsewhere.

The realisation, when it came, wasn't dramatic. It was quiet and unsettling: I had learned how to live with noise, but I had not learned how to turn it down.

Tolerance had replaced care. Endurance had replaced regulation.

That realisation didn't solve the problem, but it reframed it. The goal was no longer to eliminate noise entirely—that's unrealistic. The goal was to create deliberate intervals where noise could not survive. Where attention was fully claimed by something real, immediate, and consequential.

At that point, I didn't yet know what that would be.

I only knew that whatever came next would need to *demand* presence, not merely suggest it. It would need to leave no room for rumination. No space for mental multitasking. It would need to be honest in its feedback and indifferent to excuses.

Noise thrives in ambiguity.

It dissolves under responsibility.

The chapters that follow trace how that understanding led me—almost accidentally—toward riding, and how riding became not an escape from mental noise, but a disciplined interruption of it.

Not a cure.

A correction.

3

MAINTENANCE, NOT REPAIR

"Every habit and faculty is preserved and increased by corresponding actions."

— *Epictetus*

One of the quiet reasons many men resist mental health work is the language used to describe it.

We talk about being *broken*. About needing to be *fixed*. About returning to some earlier version of ourselves, as though there was a time when everything functioned effortlessly and without strain. For men who are still working, providing, and showing up, this framing often feels exaggerated or irrelevant.

If nothing is obviously broken, why seek repair?

The problem is that mental health does not operate on a binary. It is not broken or whole. It is a system under load. And like any system under sustained load, it degrades gradually if it is not maintained.

Nothing dramatic announces this degradation.

Attention dulls slightly. Patience thins. Recovery takes longer. Small irritations linger. You compensate, adjust, and carry on. From the outside, nothing appears wrong. From the inside, everything feels heavier than it should.

I didn't recognise this as a mental health issue at first because it didn't match the stories I had absorbed. Mental health, as it is often presented, arrives with crisis, diagnosis, or visible dysfunction. What I was experiencing was subtler and therefore easier to dismiss.

I wasn't failing. I was wearing down.

Maintenance offered a different way of understanding what was happening.

Maintenance does not imply failure. It assumes responsibility. It acknowledges that complexity requires care and that ongoing demand without counterbalance produces strain. A machine that is maintained lasts longer. A body that is trained and rested performs better. A mind that is attended to remains reliable under pressure.

This is not indulgence. It is competence.

Men accept this logic almost everywhere except internally. We service vehicles. We maintain tools. We update skills. We plan finances. We replace parts before failure when we're being sensible. Yet many of us treat our mental state as something that should simply endure whatever life applies to it.

That assumption is neither stoic nor strong. It is careless.

What made this harder to recognise was that endurance had worked for a long time. I had learned to carry stress quietly. To absorb pressure without complaint. To function even when things felt crowded internally. That ability was rewarded. It became part of how I understood myself.

But endurance is not the same as sustainability.

A system can function while degrading. It can continue to perform while its margins shrink. And because collapse has not yet occurred, we mistake continuation for health.

This is where the repair mindset becomes dangerous.

If you wait for something to break before acting, you guarantee unnecessary damage. You also train yourself to ignore early indicators. You dismiss fatigue as weakness. You interpret irritability as attitude. You treat restlessness as a lack of discipline.

Maintenance asks different questions.

Not *What's wrong?* But *What is being asked of this system, and is it being supported accordingly?*

When I began asking that question honestly, the answer was clear. My life required sustained attention, judgement, and emotional regulation. What it did not include—at least deliberately—was any structured practice that maintained those capacities.

Rest alone was not enough.

Rest without structure often became rumination. Leisure without boundaries became distraction. Silence without engagement allowed noise to resurface. I could stop moving, but I couldn't stop bracing.

What I needed was not less responsibility, but a way to support carrying it.

This is where structure matters.

Structure reduces cognitive load. It clarifies what is required and when. It narrows choices and makes consequences visible. Philosophically, structure aligns intention with action.

Psychologically, it allows the mind to stand down because it knows what is expected of it.

Without structure, even good intentions scatter.

Many modern approaches to mental health emphasise expression, which has its place. But for men who process experience through action, competence-based regulation is often more stabilising. Doing something that demands focus, skill, and responsibility can regulate the nervous system more reliably than talking alone.

Maintenance, in this sense, is active.

It is choosing practices that keep internal systems calibrated under load. It is noticing early signs of strain and responding before failure occurs. It is understanding that strength includes foresight, not just tolerance.

This reframing changed how I evaluated potential solutions.

I stopped looking for relief. Relief is temporary. It dulls sensation without restoring capacity. I started looking for alignment—something that would integrate attention, responsibility, and consequence rather than remove them.

I didn't yet see motorcycles as that solution.

At the time, riding appeared practical. Interesting. Perhaps even recreational. What I did not realise was that riding would introduce a form of disciplined maintenance I had been missing—one that demanded presence, rewarded care, and punished neglect honestly and without drama.

That comes later.

For now, the point is this: mental health does not need to be dramatic to deserve attention. It does not need to be broken to require care. And it does not improve simply by being endured.

Maintenance is not weakness. It is maturity.

Maturity—whether in philosophy, riding, or life—is what allows complexity to be handled without collapse.

4

WHY I STARTED RIDING

"First say to yourself what you would be; and then do what you have to do."

— *Epictetus*

I did not start riding because I was searching for myself.

There was no crisis, no rebellion, no dramatic turning point that pushed me toward a motorcycle. The decision emerged quietly, shaped less by emotion than by curiosity. Riding looked demanding. It required skill, attention, and judgement. It carried consequence. That combination made it compelling.

What I did not anticipate was how exposing it would feel to begin.

As adults, we spend years accumulating competence. We learn how to move through the world efficiently. We build routines, habits, and roles that allow us to operate with a degree of confidence. Over time, that competence becomes stabilising—not just practically, but psychologically. We know who we are because we know what we can do.

Learning to ride disrupted that sense of certainty.

Suddenly, I was inexperienced in a domain where inexperience mattered. Motorcycles do not tolerate vague understanding or assumed competence. You either know what you are doing or you do not, and the consequences are immediate. This made the early stages of learning both humbling and confronting.

It also made me cautious.

The idea of riding on open roads did not initially feel liberating. It felt exposed. Sitting there with the bike idling beneath me, helmet on, visor down, I was acutely aware of traffic, speed, and the thinness of the margin for error. Cars felt larger. Movement felt faster. The road felt less forgiving than it does from behind a windscreen.

This wasn't panic. It was respect.

Respect for consequence sharpens judgement. It slows you down in the right way. I did not want to rush past that feeling. I wanted to understand it, and to enter the road deliberately rather than bravely.

Training made that unavoidable.

There is something uniquely uncomfortable about being visibly unskilled as an adult. You cannot intellectualise your way out of it. You cannot hide behind experience from other areas of life. Balance, coordination, and timing reveal themselves immediately.

For me, this was most obvious in slow-speed manoeuvres.

I was particularly bad at U-turns.

Tight turns expose everything at once: balance, throttle control, clutch modulation, where your eyes are going, and how much tension you're carrying. I overthought them. I hesitated. I tried to control the bike rather than work with it. Each attempt made the gap between intention and execution uncomfortably visible.

It was frustrating, but also instructive.

U-turns taught me something quickly: force does not substitute for fluency. You cannot bully a motorcycle into compliance. You have to trust momentum, trust balance, and commit to the movement. Half-measures make things worse.

This ran directly against instincts that had served me well elsewhere.

As adults, we rely heavily on decisiveness, self-reliance, and control. On a motorcycle, especially as a beginner, those instincts can become liabilities. Confidence without skill destabilises. Hesitation creates instability. Trying to manage everything consciously overwhelms attention.

Learning required letting go of habits I was accustomed to relying on.

The most difficult part was allowing myself to trust my instructor's judgement.

From my perspective, my shortcomings were obvious. My discomfort was obvious. I felt unready to progress. From the instructor's perspective, something else was visible: enough control, enough awareness, enough consistency to justify moving forward.

Being told I was ready when I did not feel ready created a tension I wasn't used to sitting with.

As an adult, you are rarely asked to trust someone else's assessment of your competence so directly. We prefer internal readiness. Riding demanded external standards. To continue, I had to accept that my discomfort was not a reliable indicator of incapacity.

That required humility.

Not the performative kind that announces itself, but the practical kind that says, *I don't feel ready, but I am willing to trust the process.* That trust was not blind. It was structured. It rested on clear instruction, repeated practice, and immediate feedback.

Over time, that trust paid off.

The road did not become less dangerous. I simply became more capable. Attention sharpened. Movements smoothed out. The bike felt less foreign beneath me. Apprehension receded—not replaced by bravado, but by familiarity.

Familiarity, I learned, is earned slowly.

Each clean stop. Each controlled turn. Each moment where the bike responded correctly without conscious strain. These moments accumulated quietly, until competence felt less like something I was pretending to have and more like something I was building.

The humility required to learn began to feel stabilising rather than threatening.

Accepting limits reduced internal friction. Focusing on fundamentals quieted mental noise. Improvement became measurable. Progress was earned, not asserted.

This extended beyond riding.

There is dignity in submitting to competence. In allowing yourself to be shaped by standards rather than insisting on self-definition. In recognising that not knowing is not a flaw, but a starting point.

Riding did not remove responsibility from my life. It added to it. Fatigue had to be respected. Preparation mattered. Maintenance became non-negotiable. The bike demanded seriousness, not performance.

In this way, riding aligned with how I already understood adulthood. Freedom was not the absence of constraint. It was the result of disciplined engagement with reality.

I did not start riding to escape my life.

I started riding because it asked something of me that life was already asking—but in a form that was clear, embodied, and honest.

The first motorcycle would make these lessons tangible in ways instruction alone could not.

5

THE FIRST MOTORCYCLE

"The happiness of your life depends upon the quality of your thoughts."

— *Marcus Aurelius*

Choosing a first motorcycle feels deceptively practical.

People talk about engine size, seat height, reliability, resale. All of that matters, especially at the beginning. But those considerations sit on the surface. Underneath them is a quieter decision—one most riders don't articulate at the time. You are choosing not just a machine, but a way of engaging with risk, attention, and responsibility.

In that sense, the first bike is rarely accidental.

My first motorcycle was a Benelli 502C.

I named her "Nelli". Nelli the Benelli.

In Perth—and in Australia more broadly—that choice raised eyebrows. Benelli isn't a common badge on local roads, and the 502C is an outlier even within Benelli's own range. It's not a sports bike. It's not a traditional cruiser. It doesn't sit neatly in any popular category. It looks deliberate rather than aggressive. Composed rather than urgent.

That mattered to me more than I realised at the time.

Choosing something uncommon meant stepping outside a ready-made narrative. There was no dominant culture telling me how the bike should be ridden, what it said about me, or how I was meant to feel on it. The relationship between rider and machine felt quieter, more personal. Less about image. More about fit.

And fit was what I was looking for.

Nelli's design is unmistakably Italian—long, low, and elegant—but her behaviour is grounded. The riding position doesn't encourage posturing. You sit *in* the bike, not on top of it. That changes how you move. It changes how you think. Riding feels less like chasing sensation and more like occupying space deliberately.

The parallel-twin engine suited me immediately. Smooth. Predictable. Not explosive. It didn't reward impatience or punish restraint. Throttle input mattered. Gear choice mattered. Smoothness mattered. If you rushed, the bike let you know. If you settled, it responded in kind.

That honesty was important.

As a new rider, I wasn't interested in a machine that made me feel more capable than I actually was. I didn't want confidence to get ahead of competence. I wanted a bike that reinforced good habits and made bad ones uncomfortable—not dangerous, but obvious.

Nelli did that consistently.

Her weight, often criticised in reviews, worked in my favour. At low speeds she demanded attention. You couldn't be casual with her. You couldn't drift mentally. Balance mattered. Planning mattered. Inputs had to be deliberate. In return, she offered stability and a sense of being grounded rather than perched.

That dynamic mirrored something internal.

At that stage of my life, I didn't need amplification. I needed steadiness. I needed something that slowed me down without dulling me. Nelli required engagement without agitation. Riding her felt like cooperating with physics rather than trying to dominate it.

Motorcycles shape behaviour more than riders like to admit.

A powerful bike invites excess unless discipline intervenes. A twitchy bike invites tension. A light bike can invite laziness. Nelli invited attentiveness. She rewarded riding *well*, not riding *loudly*. That distinction is subtle, but it matters.

Over time, I noticed how that carried over mentally.

The calmer I rode, the quieter my head became. Smooth inputs produced smooth outcomes. Careless moments felt awkward rather than thrilling. Without being framed as such, the bike was teaching regulation. It was reinforcing the idea that restraint produces better results than force.

There was also something quietly affirming about riding a bike few others had chosen.

Owning a Benelli 502C meant I wasn't constantly measuring myself against a local standard. There was no pressure to keep up with a particular image. The bike didn't ask me to prove anything. It simply asked me to pay attention.

That mattered.

The machine you choose reflects what you value. Speed or steadiness. Conformity or independence. Image or substance. Nelli reflected a preference for competence over spectacle. A comfort with standing slightly outside the mainstream—not to be different for its own sake, but to be aligned.

She also reflected responsibility.

Nelli demanded maintenance. Chain tension. Tyre pressure. Fluids. Wear. None of it could be ignored. Neglect announced itself quickly. Care paid dividends. This reinforced a mental framework that was already forming: systems function best when they are maintained deliberately rather than repaired reactively.

There is an intimacy that develops with a first motorcycle that never quite repeats.

Every sound feels significant. Every vibration is noticed. You learn the machine's tolerances and moods. You listen more closely. You ride more attentively. That attentiveness begins to bleed into other areas of life—not because you try to transfer it, but because it becomes habitual.

Over time, Nelli stopped feeling like an unusual choice and started feeling inevitable.

She wasn't the bike most people would have chosen for me. But she was the bike that made sense for how I wanted to ride, and for who I was becoming. She didn't promise transformation. She offered consistency. She didn't amplify emotion. She steadied it.

And in retrospect, that is exactly what a first motorcycle should do.

It should not overwhelm you. It should not flatter you. It should teach you who you are when discipline, responsibility, and attention are required at the same time.

Nelli did that quietly, without spectacle, and without apology.

And in doing so, she confirmed something I've come to believe more strongly with every ride: the way you ride—and the machine you choose to do it on—reveals far more about you than the story you tell about yourself.

6

Ego Machina

"No man is free who is not master of himself." — *Epictetus*

If the first motorcycle teaches you how to ride, it also begins to reveal how you see yourself.

Not in obvious ways. Not in slogans or declarations. But in subtler patterns. In what draws you in. In what feels excessive. In what feels unnecessary. In what feels right.

We rarely admit that machinery carries psychological weight. We prefer to frame our choices as practical. But motorcycles are not purely functional objects. They are visible, expressive, and inseparable from the rider while in motion. When you ride, the machine becomes part of your silhouette. It shapes how others see you—and how you see yourself.

If I'm honest, I didn't choose Nelli for status or speed. I chose her because she felt balanced. And balance has been the work of my adult life—not intensity, not dominance, but steadiness under load.

That makes it more than transport.

Carl Jung wrote about the persona—the mask a person presents to the world in order to operate within it. The persona is not inherently false. It is often necessary. But it can become rigid. It can harden into identity. And when that happens, the individual begins to serve the mask rather than the other way around.

Motorcycles can quietly attach themselves to that mask.

Some riders are drawn to dominance—machines that command space and volume. Some are drawn to speed—precision, aggression, forward pressure. Others lean toward heritage—tradition, lineage, tribe. Some choose minimalism—stripped back, utilitarian, almost monastic.

None of these inclinations are wrong. But they are rarely random.

A motorcycle can express alignment. It can also compensate for insecurity. It can amplify confidence that already exists, or attempt to manufacture confidence that does not. It can become a form of armour—something that signals certainty in moments when certainty feels fragile.

The distinction is internal.

If the bike is chosen to complete you, it will eventually expose the gap. If it is chosen to express you, it will refine what is already present.

This is where identity becomes important.

Masculinity often drifts toward performance. Toward visible markers of strength. Toward shorthand signals that require no explanation. A powerful machine can function as one of those signals. It can say something before you do.

But signals are not substance.

If the machine becomes the identity, then identity becomes conditional. Dependent. Vulnerable to loss. A sale, a breakdown, an accident—and suddenly something structural feels removed.

A healthier posture is quieter.

The motorcycle should not define the man. It should reveal him.

That revelation often happens in small ways. In how a rider responds to frustration. In how he reacts to being overtaken. In whether he pushes beyond his limits to impress or settles into a pace that reflects his own judgement. The bike becomes a mirror under pressure.

It exposes impatience.

It exposes ego.

It exposes insecurity.

It also exposes discipline.

It exposes humility.

It exposes steadiness.

The machine does not create these qualities. It magnifies them.

This is why the question is never, "What bike should a man ride?" The better question is, "Why does this one feel right to him?"

Over time, I came to understand that what drew me to an uncommon machine was not rebellion. It was independence without hostility. It was a desire to ride without inheriting a script. I didn't want a ready-made identity. I wanted room to develop my own.

That difference matters.

Choosing something slightly outside the dominant narrative meant I had to decide what riding meant for me. There was no cultural shorthand to hide behind. No aesthetic to adopt wholesale. The relationship remained direct—between rider, machine, and road.

That directness mirrors something larger.

Individuation—another Jungian idea—is the process of becoming integrated rather than performed. It is the slow work of aligning the inner self with outward action. Riding can accelerate that process, not because it transforms you, but because it removes certain distractions. Under the helmet, performance has less oxygen.

There is no audience.

There is only input and consequence.

Over time, the machine becomes less of a symbol and more of a practice. It stops signalling and starts shaping. It refines judgement. It reinforces habits. It demands congruence between thought and action.

When that happens, identity stabilises.

The motorcycle is no longer armour. It is no longer a costume; it becomes an extension of a temperament already forming—not an attempt to manufacture one.

And perhaps that is the most honest measure of whether the machine fits: not how loudly it announces you, but how little you need to explain yourself while riding it.

A man should be able to step off his motorcycle and remain whole.

If the machine leaves, the character should remain.

If the identity collapses without the bike, then the bike was carrying too much.

But if the motorcycle simply expressed what was already steady—if it refined rather than replaced—then the relationship has been healthy.

In the end, the machine does not make the man.

It makes him visible.

7

EARLY LESSONS IN RISK

"He who fears death will never do anything worth of a living man."

— *Seneca*

Risk announces itself quickly on a motorcycle.

Not dramatically, and not always loudly—but clearly enough that it cannot be ignored. From the earliest rides, it becomes obvious that the margins are thinner than in most areas of adult life. Mistakes that would be trivial elsewhere carry weight here. Inattention is not abstract. Overconfidence is not theoretical.

This was confronting in a useful way.

Before riding, I thought of myself as cautious. Responsible. Measured. Riding tested those assumptions. It exposed the difference between *believing* you respect risk and *demonstrating* that respect moment by moment.

On the bike, there is nowhere for illusion to hide.

Nelli made this clear early on. Her weight, balance, and geometry didn't allow careless movement. Low-speed riding demanded intention. Poor lines felt awkward. Hesitation destabilised balance. The bike responded honestly to what I did, not to what I intended.

The first lesson was humility.

I learned quickly that confidence does not reduce risk—competence does. And competence is slow. It is built through repetition, correction, and restraint. Each ride revealed small gaps in skill that no amount of optimism could conceal.

This was uncomfortable, but clarifying.

Many men carry confidence as a default posture. It serves us well in leadership, decision-making, and problem-solving. On a motorcycle, however, confidence untethered from skill becomes a liability. The bike does not care how sure you feel. It responds only to input and physics.

That honesty reshapes behaviour.

One of the most important early lessons was learning to respect limits—both the bike's and my own. Fatigue mattered more than I wanted it to. Distraction narrowed awareness faster than expected. Riding when mentally crowded felt different, and not in a good way.

Pushing through did not create growth. It created instability.

This forced a reconsideration of how I understood risk.

There is a persistent idea that growth happens at the edge of danger. Riding taught me the opposite. Progress comes from expanding margins gradually, not from flirting with their collapse. Risk is not something to conquer. It is something to manage.

That distinction matters beyond the bike.

Masculinity is often framed in terms of risk-taking, but rarely in terms of risk assessment. Courage is confused with recklessness.

Assertiveness is mistaken for disregard. Riding makes this confusion unsustainable.

Every decision on the bike has downstream consequences.

A misjudgement doesn't end with me. It ripples outward—to the people who expect me home, to the responsibilities waiting off the road, to lives that intersect briefly with mine in traffic. Riding made responsibility concrete rather than abstract.

This changed how I evaluated "worthwhile" risk.

The question was no longer *Can I do this?* but *Should I?* That shift sounds small, but it alters behaviour fundamentally. It replaces ego with judgement. It reframes restraint as strength rather than hesitation.

There were moments early on when ego surfaced quietly.

The temptation to keep pace with more experienced riders. The urge to push slightly harder than necessary. The subtle desire to demonstrate competence before it was earned. None of this was dramatic. It was internal, rationalised, easy to justify.

Nelli corrected these impulses without theatrics.

Rough inputs felt rough. Poor decisions felt unstable. Smooth riding felt calm. Over time, I learned to associate steadiness with safety, and safety with confidence. The bike trained me to trust restraint.

That recalibration extended inward.

I began to see parallels between riding risk and psychological risk. Both involve exposure. Both require judgement. Both punish denial. Avoidance creates fragility. Recklessness creates harm. Stability emerges from measured engagement.

Risk, when approached properly, clarifies values.

Riding made it impossible to pretend that freedom exists without consequence. Every moment of movement was borrowed against attention, skill, and care. The ride was enjoyable because of the discipline beneath it, not despite it.

This reframed how I thought about freedom more broadly.

Freedom was not doing whatever I felt like in the moment. It was doing what I could sustain. It was choosing actions that preserved capacity rather than depleted it. It was understanding that responsibility is not a constraint on freedom, but its precondition.

The early lessons of riding were not thrilling.

They were quiet. Repetitive. Occasionally frustrating. But they were honest. They taught me that risk is not something to chase for intensity. It is something to engage with deliberately, respectfully, and with full awareness of what is at stake.

Those lessons would deepen over time and shape how I thought about masculinity, responsibility, and mental health in ways that extended far beyond the bike.

But they began simply, and insistently, with Nelli reminding me—ride after ride—that competence is earned, restraint is strength, and risk is never abstract.

8

WHY RISK APPEALS TO MEN

"Difficulties strengthen the mind, as labor does the body."

— Seneca

Risk appeals to men not because men are careless, but because risk clarifies reality.

In a world that is increasingly abstract—mediated by screens, policies, procedures, and endless interpretation—risk collapses complexity into decision. You act, and something happens. There is no committee. No delay. No ambiguity about whether your choices matter.

For many men, that clarity is deeply stabilising.

Risk demands presence. It narrows attention. It pulls the mind out of speculation and back into the body. When risk is real, thought aligns with action. This alignment is rare in modern life, and its absence leaves many men restless without knowing why.

This is not about thrill-seeking.

The stereotype of men chasing danger for excitement alone misunderstands the attraction. What most men are responding to is not danger, but consequence. Risk introduces stakes.

Stakes give weight to action. Weight restores seriousness to behaviour.

Riding makes this visible immediately.

On a motorcycle, risk is present but bounded. It is not chaos. It is structured exposure. Skill reduces danger. Attention widens margins. Discipline expands what is possible. The rider is not reckless by default; he is accountable by design.

This accountability is grounding.

In many areas of adult life, standards are diffuse. Expectations shift. Outcomes are negotiated. Feedback is delayed or softened. It becomes difficult to know whether you are doing well or merely staying afloat.

Risk removes that ambiguity.

On the bike, inputs are clear. Consequences follow. The feedback is immediate and honest. You are either smooth or you are not. Attentive or distracted. Prepared or careless. There is relief in that clarity.

This has implications for masculinity.

Men often calibrate identity through competence under pressure. When there is no legitimate pressure, competence becomes theoretical. It exists in stories and intentions rather than behaviour. Risk provides a context where judgement must be demonstrated, not asserted.

This is why removing risk entirely does not eliminate the impulse toward it.

When men lack constructive avenues to engage risk, they often seek substitutes. Overwork. Conflict. Emotional withdrawal.

Excessive self-reliance. These are risks too—just unmanaged and unacknowledged. They erode rather than build.

Riding offers something different.

It channels the appetite for risk into a discipline that rewards care, not bravado. It demands preparation. It punishes inattention. It teaches proportion. Risk is not eliminated; it is educated.

This education reshapes behaviour.

I noticed that when risk was structured, I felt calmer rather than agitated. The presence of consequence did not increase anxiety; it reduced it. The mind settled because it knew what was required. Attention became selective. Irrelevant concerns fell away.

Risk, engaged properly, quiets the mind.

This may seem counterintuitive, but it makes sense. Anxiety thrives in ambiguity. Risk, when bounded by competence and responsibility, replaces ambiguity with clarity. The question is no longer *What if?* but *What now?*

That shift is stabilising.

Risk also restores a sense of agency that can be missing in modern life. Many men feel acted upon—by systems, expectations, and obligations they did not choose. Risk reintroduces choice with consequence. You decide. You act. You own the outcome.

This ownership matters.

It fosters responsibility rather than entitlement. It encourages preparation rather than complaint. It rewards restraint rather than impulse. These are not accidental by-products; they are inherent to competent engagement with risk.

But here is the crucial distinction: risk is not the same as recklessness.

Recklessness seeks sensation. Risk seeks engagement. Recklessness ignores consequence. Risk acknowledges it. Recklessness inflates the ego. Risk humbles it.

Understanding why risk appeals to men allows us to reclaim it from caricature.

Risk is not a flaw to be eliminated. It is a force to be educated. The goal is not safety at all costs, nor danger for its own sake. The goal is a life where risk is acknowledged, respected, and integrated into a broader framework of responsibility.

Riding taught me that when risk is approached seriously, it does not destabilise you. It steadies you.

It anchors attention. It clarifies values. It restores proportion.

And when risk is engaged well, it stops being something you chase—and becomes something you manage.

That is the difference between appetite and discipline.

And it is a difference worth learning.

9

Recklessness Is Not Courage

"Don't explain your philosophy. Embody it."

— *Epictetus*

Recklessness often passes for courage because, from a distance, the two can look similar.

Both involve action. Both involve exposure. Both involve moving toward uncertainty rather than away from it. But the similarity ends there. Courage is grounded in responsibility. Recklessness is indifferent to it.

Riding makes this distinction unavoidable.

On a motorcycle, courage does not announce itself. It does not seek witnesses. It does not require intensity to validate it. Courage shows up in preparation, judgement, and restraint. It appears in decisions that are boring to describe but critical to survival.

Recklessness wants to be felt.

It mistakes adrenaline for meaning and speed for confidence. It treats limits as insults and warnings as challenges. From the outside, it can look impressive. From the inside, it is usually reactive and poorly considered.

The road does not reward that for long.

Early on, I became aware of how easy it would be to confuse the two. The temptation was subtle. A slightly faster corner than necessary. Staying out longer when fatigue was already present. Ignoring small signals because nothing had gone wrong *yet*. None of this felt dramatic. It felt justifiable.

That's how recklessness usually enters.

It rarely announces itself as stupidity. It presents as optimism. As confidence. As "I've got this." The danger is not in bold action, but in action detached from judgement.

Riding corrected this gently, but persistently.

When I rode smoothly, things felt calm. When I rushed, they felt unstable. When I respected limits, the ride opened up. When I ignored them, margins shrank quickly. Over time, I learned that the bike wasn't restricting me—it was teaching me.

Courage, I realised, is cumulative.

It is built through repeated acts of restraint that preserve capacity over time. It looks like riding within yourself even when you could push harder. It looks like stopping when concentration fades. It looks like choosing longevity over spectacle.

Recklessness, by contrast, is consumptive.

It burns resources without replenishing them. It trades tomorrow's stability for today's intensity. It feels powerful in the moment, but leaves you diminished afterward—physically, mentally, or both.

This distinction matters far beyond riding.

Many men engage recklessly with their own limits while believing they are being strong. They override fatigue. They ignore stress signals. They push through situations that require adjustment rather than endurance. When this behaviour is praised as grit, it becomes self-reinforcing.

But grit without judgement is erosion.

Courage involves facing discomfort without abandoning responsibility. It includes asking for help when it is required, changing course when conditions shift, and recognising when persistence has become avoidance.

Recklessness refuses these corrections. It doubles down. It treats every warning as a test of character rather than information.

There is also an ego component here that deserves honesty.

Recklessness often emerges when identity becomes tied to performance rather than character. When being seen as bold matters more than being reliable, restraint feels like a threat. In environments where masculinity is measured by visibility rather than contribution, this confusion becomes common.

Riding strips that illusion away.

The motorcycle does not care about your self-image. It responds only to physics and input. It reflects behaviour without commentary. It becomes a mirror—not of who you claim to be, but of how you actually act under pressure.

That feedback is fair, if unforgiving.

Over time, I learned to associate calm with courage. Smoothness with competence. Conservative decisions with strength. Riding well felt less like asserting myself and more like cooperating with reality.

That cooperation is what courage looks like when stripped of theatrics.

There is nothing weak about restraint. There is nothing timid about patience. There is nothing passive about choosing sustainability over spectacle. These are not concessions. They are commitments.

The romanticisation of recklessness has done men no favours.

It has encouraged short-term intensity at the expense of long-term stability. It has confused fearlessness with wisdom and dismissed caution as fragility. In truth, caution is simply respect for consequence.

Respect is not fear.

Courage allows you to engage risk without being consumed by it. Recklessness invites risk without understanding it. One builds capacity. The other depletes it.

Riding taught me that the difference between the two is not philosophical. It is behavioural. It shows up in habits, preparation, and judgement. It shows up in whether you return home intact.

Ultimately, courage is a form of stewardship.

It is stewardship of your body, your attention, and the people who rely on your presence. Recklessness abdicates that stewardship in pursuit of momentary intensity.

If masculinity is to mean anything durable, it must make this distinction clear.

Courage endures.

Recklessness burns out.

The road makes that lesson unavoidable.

10

RESPONSIBILITY AS STRENGTH

"Waste no more time arguing about what a good man should be. Be one."

— *Marcus Aurelius*

Responsibility is often spoken about as though it is something that diminishes freedom.

It is framed as obligation, constraint, or sacrifice—necessary, perhaps, but undesirable. In this framing, freedom exists only where responsibility is absent, and adulthood becomes a slow narrowing of possibility rather than an expansion of capacity.

This framing is wrong.

Responsibility, when properly understood, is not the enemy of freedom. It is the condition that makes freedom sustainable.

Riding makes this obvious in a way few other experiences do.

On a motorcycle, you are free to ride because you have already accepted responsibility—responsibility for preparation, maintenance, judgement, and restraint. The ride exists because the work has been done beforehand. Remove that responsibility, and what remains is not freedom, but chaos.

This is not philosophical. It is practical.

Every ride is underwritten by responsibility. Tyres checked. Chain maintained. Fatigue assessed honestly. Conditions read correctly. These are not constraints on freedom; they are what make movement possible at all.

The same is true off the bike.

Masculinity, at its best, is expressed through stewardship. Stewardship of one's body, one's skills, one's commitments, and one's impact on others. A man who accepts responsibility does not shrink his life—he stabilises it.

That stability matters psychologically.

When responsibility is owned rather than resented, internal friction reduces. Decisions align with values. Attention stops scattering. Life feels demanding, but not chaotic. The constant low-level tension that comes from avoiding obligation begins to ease.

Riding reinforced this for me quietly, ride after ride.

Nelli demanded responsibility consistently, not occasionally. Maintenance could not be deferred indefinitely. Fatigue could not be ignored without consequence. Riding "how I felt" rather than how conditions required never ended well. These were not punishments. They were reminders.

And in meeting those reminders, something unexpected happened.

Riding felt liberating.

The freedom of the ride was not despite responsibility—it was because of it. Knowing the machine was sound, knowing my judgement was intact, knowing my limits were respected allowed me to ride with confidence rather than tension.

That same principle applies inwardly.

When responsibility is avoided, it does not disappear. It migrates. It becomes anxiety. It becomes irritability. It becomes background noise. When responsibility is claimed, it becomes grounding.

This stands in contrast to a cultural narrative that treats responsibility as an imposition.

When men internalise that narrative, they often resist commitment, delay maintenance—internal and external—and chase autonomy in ways that undermine their own stability. The result is a brittle freedom that collapses under pressure.

Responsibility, by contrast, thickens identity.

It anchors self-worth in reliability rather than performance. It shifts focus from being seen to being useful. It rewards foresight, patience, and care—qualities that compound quietly over time.

These qualities are not glamorous. They do not trend. But they endure.

There is also an ethical dimension here that riding makes impossible to ignore.

Every decision on a motorcycle implicates others. Drivers. Pedestrians. Family members waiting at home. Riding well is not only a personal achievement; it is a moral act. It is a recognition that your choices ripple outward.

That awareness reshaped how I thought about responsibility more broadly.

The question stopped being *What do I want right now?* and became *What is required of me here?* That shift is subtle, but foundational. It replaces impulse with judgement and reaction with intention.

In mental health terms, this is stabilising.

Men who view responsibility as strength tend to experience greater internal coherence. They are less likely to oscillate between excess and withdrawal. They understand that care is not indulgence and that limits are not failures.

Riding crystallised this because it allowed no illusions.

You cannot outsource responsibility on a motorcycle. You cannot blame conditions you failed to assess or maintenance you neglected. The feedback is immediate and impartial. The ride tells the truth.

That honesty is refreshing.

It is also demanding.

Maturity is not about having fewer desires. It is about ordering them properly. It is the ability to subordinate impulse to judgement without feeling diminished by the act. Responsibility makes this possible by providing a framework in which choice retains meaning.

Without responsibility, choice becomes noise.

This is why responsibility should be reclaimed as a masculine virtue rather than endured as a burden. It is what allows men to engage deeply without becoming reckless, and to care without becoming fragile.

Responsibility does not limit the man.

It defines him.

On the bike and off it, the strongest moments are rarely the loudest ones. They are the quiet decisions made consistently over time—the choice to prepare, to restrain, to maintain, and to return home intact.

That is strength with substance.

And it lasts.

11

WHAT RIDING REGULATES

"The soul becomes dyed with the colour of its thoughts."

— *Marcus Aurelius*

Riding did not fix my problems.

That matters enough to say plainly.

There is a temptation—especially in conversations about men, mental health, and motorcycles—to frame riding as a cure. As therapy by other means. As something that replaces the harder work of reflection, conversation, or change. That narrative is appealing, but it is false.

What riding did for me was quieter, and more reliable.

It regulated.

Before riding, my mental state was not dramatic. I wasn't in crisis. I was functioning—working, meeting obligations, showing up where I needed to. But internally, things felt compressed. Thoughts overlapped. Decisions lingered longer than they should have. Even when nothing was "wrong," my mind rarely felt settled.

Riding changed the quality of my attention.

On the bike, there was no room for background noise. I could not replay conversations while cornering. I could not rehearse worries while managing traffic, surface conditions, speed, and position. The road demanded everything at once.

That fullness was calming.

It wasn't distraction. Distraction pulls you away from yourself. Riding pulled me fully into the moment. The difference became obvious after rides. I would come home and notice that my thoughts were clearer, more proportionate. Problems that had felt heavy earlier in the day were still there, but they no longer crowded one another.

I could think again.

Riding also regulated my physiological state in ways I didn't expect. From the outside, motorcycles look overstimulating. From the inside, competent riding is controlled and deliberate. Breathing slows. Movements become economical. The body is alert without being agitated.

That mattered, because I had grown used to carrying tension as a baseline.

Before riding, rest rarely felt restorative. Sitting still often meant rumination. Silence invited mental rehearsal. Riding imposed a different rhythm. It contained attention. It gave my nervous system a clear job to do—and just as importantly, permission to stop doing everything else.

Over time, I began to trust this effect.

Riding also restored a sense of competence at a point where much of life felt abstract. Progress on the bike was tangible. I could feel improvements in smoothness, judgement, and control. These gains were earned, not imagined. They reminded me that capability still existed, even when mental clarity felt inconsistent elsewhere.

That mattered more than motivation ever did.

There was also a subtle identity shift that occurred without ceremony. On the bike, I was not a collection of roles or obligations. I was simply a rider, responsible for what was in front of me. That simplicity wasn't escapism—it was relief from fragmentation.

For a while, that relief felt sufficient.

But honesty requires limits.

Riding regulated my mental state. It did not resolve what sat underneath it. It quieted the noise, but it did not answer why the noise existed. It created space, but it did not fill that space with meaning or direction.

When the helmet came off, life resumed.

This is where riding can be misunderstood.

If riding becomes the only place you feel ordered, it risks becoming avoidance. I became aware of this gradually. There were moments when I noticed the temptation to ride instead of addressing something difficult. Riding made things bearable—but bearable is not the same as resolved.

That distinction matters.

Riding is at its best when it supports mental health, not when it replaces the work required elsewhere. It gives clarity, but clarity still demands action. It steadies the system, but steadiness is only useful if it leads to better judgement off the bike.

Used well, riding regulated my attention, my arousal, and my sense of agency. It gave me back a mental baseline from which I could function deliberately rather than reactively.

Used poorly, it could have become a refuge I never left.

Understanding that boundary was essential.

Riding did not heal me. It made me more capable of engaging honestly with what needed attention. It created the conditions for reflection, not the conclusion of it.

That is the role it should play.

Riding gives you back a steadier mind. What you do with that steadiness remains your responsibility.

And that responsibility does not disappear when the engine cools.

12

WHEN RIDING ISN'T ENOUGH

"It is impossible for a man to learn what he thinks he already knows."

— *Epictetus*

There is a point where regulation reveals its limits.

Riding can steady attention. It can quiet noise. It can return proportion to thoughts that had begun to crowd one another. But it cannot, on its own, resolve what requires naming, examination, or change.

This is not a failure of riding.

It is a boundary.

For me, that boundary did not appear as crisis. It appeared as repetition. The same thoughts resurfacing after rides. The same tensions reasserting themselves once the helmet came off. Riding made things bearable, but over time, bearable began to feel insufficient.

That realisation mattered, because it exposed the difference between support and substitution.

When riding functions well, it supports life. When it begins to substitute for something else, it quietly turns into avoidance.

Avoidance rarely announces itself as such. It often looks like discipline, commitment, or even self-care.

I noticed it in small, uncomfortable ways.

Choosing a ride when a conversation needed to happen. Preferring motion to stillness. Trusting the clarity of the road more than the ambiguity of reflection. None of this was reckless. It was understandable. Riding offered certainty. Life, at that moment, did not.

But certainty is not always what is required.

Riding had regulated me enough to see this clearly. That, in itself, was evidence of its value. But clarity creates responsibility. Once something is visible, it cannot be unseen. The question becomes what you do next.

This is where many men hesitate.

Asking for help is often framed as surrender—as though admitting limits undermines competence. In reality, refusing help when it is required erodes strength far more reliably over time.

Strength is not self-sufficiency at all costs.

It is the ability to engage the right support at the right time without abdicating responsibility. Riding had taught me restraint, judgement, and presence. Those same qualities were now required off the bike.

Talking did not come naturally.

Neither did naming internal patterns that had been managed quietly for years. It was easier to ride than to articulate what lingered underneath the calm. Easier to regulate than to integrate.

But regulation without integration eventually stalls.

Mental health work often begins here—not with collapse, but with honesty. With recognising that a coping strategy, however effective, is not the same as resolution. Riding had given me space. What I did with that space was the real work.

There is a particular courage required to step off the bike and into conversation.

It lacks the clarity of physical risk. There are no clean lines, no immediate feedback, no objective measures of progress. You don't know when you're "doing it right." You only know that it feels exposed.

But the stakes are just as real.

Mental health requires tolerating uncertainty. Sitting with discomfort without fleeing into motion. Allowing another person to see you without the buffer of competence.

This does not negate masculinity.

It matures it.

Riding did not teach me how to avoid difficulty. It taught me how to face it with steadiness. When riding stopped being enough, the answer was not to ride harder or longer. It was to listen to what the steadiness was revealing.

That listening required humility.

Not the dramatic kind. The practical kind that accepts limits without self-condemnation. That understands strength as adaptability rather than endurance alone.

Every ride ends.

The engine cools. The helmet comes off. What remains is the life you are responsible for. Riding can help you return to it with clarity, but it cannot face it for you.

That work is yours.

And recognising when riding isn't enough is not failure.

It is judgement applied inward.

13

Asking for Help Doesn't Mean You're Weak

"If someone is able to show me that what I think or do is not right, I will happily change."

— Marcus Aurelius

For a long time, the idea of counselling sat awkwardly with me.

Not because I doubted its value, but because I didn't recognise myself in the stories usually told about it. Counselling, as I understood it, belonged to crisis. To moments of collapse, loss of control, or visible dysfunction. I was still functioning. I was still reliable. I was still showing up.

It didn't feel like my place.

What changed wasn't my circumstances. It was my clarity.

Riding had regulated me enough to see patterns that had previously blended into the background. Anxiety wasn't dramatic, but it was persistent. My mind had a habit of running ahead of reality—filling uncertainty with imagined outcomes, escalating small ambiguities into disproportionate concern.

Nothing paralysed me. Nothing broke.

But the cost was constant.

Meeting with a psychologist to talk through a mental health care plan wasn't emotional. It was practical. We talked about workload, responsibility, pressure, and the way my thinking tended to move quickly toward worst-case scenarios. What stood out was how familiar these patterns felt—and how unnecessary they were.

Self-catastrophising had become habitual.

Not because I believed the worst would happen, but because my mind had learned to prepare for it automatically. Ambiguity triggered rehearsal. Uncertainty filled itself with projection. The habit wasn't irrational—it was inefficient.

Naming that mattered.

Counselling didn't invalidate my experience. It clarified it. Anxiety stopped being a vague internal weather pattern and became something observable. Trackable. Interruptible. Once it had shape, it could be addressed.

What surprised me most was how structured the process was.

There was no pressure to excavate endlessly or perform vulnerability. The focus was on mechanisms. How thoughts escalated. How physiological responses reinforced them. How attention could be redirected deliberately rather than reactively. Coping mechanisms weren't framed as emotional crutches, but as skills.

That framing made sense to me.

Learning to slow catastrophic thinking didn't involve suppressing it. It involved questioning assumptions. Separating probability from possibility. Restoring proportion. These were not foreign concepts. Riding had already been teaching me something similar.

On the bike, you assess conditions without panic. You stay alert without spiralling. You respond to what is actually in front of you, not to imagined outcomes. The same discipline applied inward.

Counselling didn't remove anxiety from my life.

It reduced its authority.

Thoughts no longer ran unchecked. The distance between trigger and response shortened. I could notice escalation sooner and intervene earlier. That alone conserved enormous mental energy.

This reframed help entirely.

I wasn't surrendering responsibility. I was exercising it. I was doing what competent people do when they encounter limits: seeking informed input to improve performance.

That is not weakness.

That is maintenance.

Just as riding taught me to respect early warning signs in a machine, counselling taught me to respect early indicators in my thinking. Ignoring them would not have proven strength. It would have guaranteed unnecessary strain.

There was also dignity in the process.

Speaking openly with a professional who did not require justification or performance allowed honesty without theatrics. I didn't need to dramatise or minimise. I simply needed to engage.

Importantly, counselling didn't replace riding.

It complemented it.

Riding regulated my system. Counselling helped me understand it. Riding created space. Counselling taught me how to use that space wisely. One without the other would have been incomplete.

This is what asking for help without abdicating strength looks like.

It is deliberate. Proportional. Purposeful. It preserves agency rather than dissolving it. It allows riding to remain what it should be—a practice that supports life, not a place to hide from it.

Strength is not diminished by seeking clarity.

It is diminished by refusing it.

Meeting with a psychologist didn't change who I was. It sharpened how I operated. It reduced unnecessary noise. It restored proportion. It made responsibility feel lighter—not because it was reduced, but because it was better managed.

That is not surrender.

That is competence applied inward.

14

ATTENTION IS THE POINT

"You become what you give your attention to."

— *Epictetus*

Everything in this book eventually returns to attention.

Not happiness. Not motivation. Not even freedom.

Attention.

Long before I had language for it, what I was struggling with was not emotion but dispersion. My attention was everywhere and nowhere at once. Split between obligations, anticipations, hypotheticals, and low-level vigilance that never quite powered down. Nothing was catastrophic. Everything was consuming.

Riding revealed this by contrast.

On the bike, attention had a single task: stay with what is happening. Speed, surface, traffic, position, balance. There was no room for rehearsal or abstraction. Thought became functional. Presence became unavoidable.

This was not accidental. It was structural.

Attention does not respond well to instruction. Telling yourself to "be present" rarely works for long. Attention responds to consequence. It settles where it is required. It stabilises when distraction is no longer an option.

Riding made that clear immediately.

Counselling clarified it further.

I began to see how easily attention could be hijacked by imagined futures, unresolved conversations, or habitual catastrophising. Most of my mental strain came not from what was happening, but from where my attention was being pulled unnecessarily.

Riding showed me what regulated attention felt like. Counselling showed me how easily it was lost.

Together, they pointed to the same truth: mental health improves when attention is governed, not indulged.

This is not about suppressing thought.

It is about discrimination. About deciding which thoughts deserve engagement and which do not. On the bike, this distinction is enforced. Irrelevant thoughts simply cannot survive. Off the bike, the discipline must be chosen.

This is where many men struggle.

Modern life trains us to treat all inputs as equally urgent. Notifications, expectations, imagined outcomes—all compete for attention. Without deliberate governance, attention fragments. When attention fragments, energy drains. When energy drains, everything feels heavier than it should.

Attention is the gateway.

Where it goes, emotion follows. Where it lingers, identity consolidates. When it is scattered, anxiety thrives. When it is anchored, proportion returns.

This is why riding felt calming rather than stimulating.

The presence of consequence narrowed focus. The mind stopped scanning for threats that didn't exist. The body and judgement aligned. The result was not adrenaline, but clarity.

That clarity mattered more than escape ever could.

Counselling added a second layer.

It taught me to notice when attention was being pulled by habit rather than necessity. To recognise catastrophising early. To slow escalation. To separate probability from possibility. To reclaim attention before it ran away with itself.

Again, this was not emotional indulgence.

It was skill acquisition.

Attention, once reclaimed, becomes selective. Not every thought needs rehearsal. Not every possibility needs planning. Not every feeling requires immediate action. Discernment restores freedom.

This is the deeper connection between riding, mental health, and philosophy.

The Stoics understood that peace comes not from controlling events, but from governing attention. Modern psychology arrives at the same conclusion through different language. Riding simply enforces it through consequence.

You do not ride to escape your life.

You ride to practise presence.

And presence, once practised, must be carried back into life deliberately.

If riding remains on the road, it becomes entertainment. If it reshapes how you attend—to conversations, decisions, relationships—it becomes discipline.

Attention is the point because it determines everything downstream.

Judgement sharpens when attention is stable. Emotion steadies. Responsibility becomes manageable. Identity stops fragmenting. Life does not become easier, but it becomes clearer.

And clarity changes how you carry weight.

The helmet goes on. The visor drops. Attention narrows.

The ride begins.

And when it ends, attention should come with you.

That is the work.

15

TAKING THE HELMET OFF

"No great thing is created suddenly."

— Epictetus

Every ride ends the same way.

The engine cools. The helmet comes off. The world returns with its noise, its demands, and its unfinished conversations. Whatever clarity the ride produced is tested immediately by what waits off the bike.

This is where the work actually begins.

It is easy to mistake the calm of riding for progress. On the road, attention is governed for you. Consequence enforces presence. Distraction has nowhere to hide. But once the helmet comes off, attention is no longer protected by structure. It must be managed deliberately.

This distinction matters.

Riding is not valuable because it removes difficulty from life. It is valuable because it shows what clarity feels like—and what is possible when attention is properly ordered. The danger is assuming that clarity belongs only on the bike.

If it does, riding becomes an escape.

I became aware of this risk slowly. There were moments when the contrast between riding and the rest of life felt too sharp. The temptation was to preserve that clarity by returning to the bike rather than carrying it forward. That impulse is understandable. It is also incomplete.

The point is not to live on the bike.

The point is to return from it differently.

What riding taught me was not how to avoid complexity, but how to engage it without scattering myself. The steadiness I felt on the road was not a product of speed or isolation. It was a product of attention governed by responsibility.

That same principle applies elsewhere.

Conversations become clearer when attention is present rather than defensive. Decisions improve when they are made deliberately rather than reactively. Anxiety loses momentum when attention is anchored in what is actually happening rather than what might.

This is harder work than riding.

There is no throttle to manage attention in daily life. No clear feedback loop. No immediate sense of rightness when things go well. The discipline is quieter and less rewarding in the short term.

But it compounds.

Taking the helmet off does not mean abandoning what riding teaches. It means translating it. The same restraint, judgement, and respect for limits that keep you safe on the road can be applied inward and outward.

Fatigue matters off the bike too.

Maintenance matters.

Preparation matters.

Attention matters.

Riding made these truths undeniable because the cost of ignoring them was immediate. Life is more forgiving—but that forgiveness often hides damage until it accumulates.

I began to see how often I ignored early indicators off the bike in ways I would never tolerate on it. Mental fatigue brushed aside. Irritability rationalised. Avoidance dressed up as busyness. Riding had trained me to notice these signals. The question was whether I would act on them.

This is where maturity shows itself.

Not in intensity. Not in performance. But in consistency. In the willingness to apply discipline when no one is watching and no immediate reward follows.

The calm that riding produces is not meant to be preserved like a souvenir. It is meant to recalibrate your baseline. To remind you what functioning well feels like so that you can recognise when you drift from it.

Taking the helmet off is not a loss.

It is a test.

A test of whether what you learn under constraint can survive without it. Whether clarity can be chosen rather than enforced. Whether attention can be governed when consequence is delayed.

Riding will always offer a place where attention is demanded and noise dissolves. That place matters. But it is not where life happens.

Life happens after the ride.

And the measure of riding's value is not how it feels in the moment, but how you live when the engine is off.

16
Returning With What Matters

"Nowhere can a man find a quieter or more untroubled retreat than in his own soul."

— *Marcus Aurelius*

Every ride teaches you something, whether you intend it to or not.

Sometimes the lesson is technical. Sometimes it is about restraint. Sometimes it is simply a reminder that attention, when governed properly, steadies the mind. But the most important lesson is not learned on the road itself.

It is learned in what you carry back with you.

Riding strips life down to essentials. Inputs matter. Consequences follow. Feedback is honest. There is no room for narrative inflation or self-deception. You do not get to pretend competence—you demonstrate it, or you don't.

This is why riding resonates so deeply with some men. It restores a form of moral clarity that is difficult to find elsewhere.

But clarity is only useful if it survives contact with ordinary life.

The temptation is to preserve riding as a separate world—a place where things make sense while the rest of life remains messy.

That temptation should be resisted. Riding is not a retreat from responsibility. It is a rehearsal for it.

What riding teaches, at its best, is not freedom from obligation but freedom through order.

The man who rides well does not ride impulsively. He prepares. He assesses conditions. He respects limits. He understands that confidence is something earned repeatedly, not declared once. He knows that care expands freedom and neglect erodes it.

These principles do not belong exclusively to riding.

They belong in conversations where restraint matters more than being right. In work where consistency outweighs performance. In family life where presence counts more than intensity. In mental health where maintenance matters more than dramatic change.

Riding sharpened my awareness of how often men are encouraged to perform strength rather than practise it. To chase intensity rather than stability. To mistake endurance for virtue.

This book has argued against that.

Strength, properly understood, is not loud. It is reliable. It is visible in how a man manages his attention, his limits, and his responsibilities over time. It shows up in preparation, maintenance, and restraint. It shows up in the willingness to ask for help without surrendering agency.

Riding did not make me a better man by itself.

It made it harder to lie to myself.

That is its greatest value.

On the bike, you learn quickly whether you are present or distracted, prepared or careless, calm or reactive. Off the bike, the same distinctions exist—they are simply easier to ignore. Riding teaches you what happens when you stop ignoring them.

The road does not demand perfection. It demands honesty.

So does life.

If you take anything from this book, let it be this: do not outsource your mental health to any single practice, including riding. Use riding to regulate yourself, not to disappear. Use philosophy to clarify responsibility, not to excuse detachment. Use masculinity to orient yourself toward stewardship, not performance.

Ride when riding helps.

Stop when stopping is required.

Talk when talking matters.

Maintain what carries you.

Eventually, the machine will wear. The body will fatigue. The mind will accumulate load. None of this is failure. It is the condition of living responsibly in the world.

What matters is whether you notice early, respond deliberately, and refuse to romanticise neglect.

The helmet comes off. The keys are set down. The world resumes.

If riding has done its work, you return not lighter, but steadier. Not invincible, but clearer. Not free of responsibility, but better equipped to carry it.

That is not escape.

That is return.

ON REFLECTION...

Hanging the Jacket on the Hook

"Begin at once to live, and count each separate day as a separate life."

— *Seneca*

If you've read this far, you already know this book isn't really about motorcycles.

It's about what happens when a man finds a place where his attention finally settles—and realises how rarely that happens elsewhere.

For me, riding became that place. Not because it fixed anything, but because it stripped things back. On the bike, there was no space to rehearse conversations or catastrophise outcomes. There was only what was in front of me, and what I chose to do with it. That simplicity mattered more than I expected.

But life doesn't stay simple.

The helmet comes off. The bike goes back in the shed. The same responsibilities wait. The same relationships need tending. The same internal habits resurface if you let them. Riding doesn't change that. What it can change is how you meet it.

I've written a lot here about discipline, responsibility, and maintenance. Those words can sound abstract until you've lived them badly for long enough to appreciate what they offer. I didn't come to them because I wanted to be austere or impressive. I came to them because they worked—and because the alternatives were quietly wearing me down.

Some days, riding is enough.

Some days, it isn't.

There were times when the calm the bike gave me showed me exactly what I'd been avoiding. Times when steadiness made it harder to ignore conversations that needed to happen or help that needed to be asked for. That was uncomfortable—but it was honest. And honesty, I've learned, is usually the beginning of improvement.

If there's anything I hope stays with you, it isn't a philosophy or a riding principle. It's the idea that strength doesn't always look like pushing harder. Sometimes it looks like noticing earlier. Adjusting sooner. Maintaining what carries you before it fails.

You don't need a motorcycle for that.

You need something—anything—that demands your full attention and gives you honest feedback in return. Something that refuses to let you hide in distraction or noise. Riding happened to be that thing for me.

When the ride ends, life resumes. It always does. The question isn't whether the world gets louder again—it will. The question is whether you carry some of that steadiness back with you, and whether you're willing to protect it.

I still ride. I still need to ride. But I've learned not to expect it to do work it can't do for me. Riding clears space. What I do with that space is my responsibility.

If this book has done anything useful, I hope it's reminded you that you don't need to be broken to take yourself seriously—and that maintenance, applied early and consistently, is one of the most practical forms of strength there is. The road will still be there tomorrow. So will the work.

There's some fuel left in the reserve...

The Dos and Don'ts of Riding

These aren't revelations. You probably already know most of what follows.

None of it is complicated, and none of it is new. In fact, that's the point. These are things riders tend to learn early, forget slowly, and relearn when something goes wrong.

I'm not offering rules or instructions here. These are reminders—the kind that only matter when they're ignored. Most bad rides don't begin with ignorance. They begin with small compromises that feel reasonable at the time.

I've written these down not because I always follow them, but because I don't always do. When I return to them, riding improves. When I don't, it usually doesn't.

Take what's useful. Leave what isn't. If any of this makes you pause before a ride, it's done its job.

Things I Don't Negotiate With...

Don't ride angry

Anger narrows attention and inflates certainty. It shortens the distance between impulse and action while convincing you judgement is still intact. Riding angry increases risk because you stop questioning decisions that should be questioned.

Don't ride tired

Fatigue lies convincingly. It doesn't announce itself as impairment; it presents as confidence. Reaction time slows, judgement blurs, and awareness narrows long before you notice.

Don't ride rushed

Time pressure quietly rewrites priorities. Decisions that would normally feel irresponsible begin to feel efficient. When I'm rushing, judgement becomes negotiable—and that's when small risks stack.

Don't ride to prove anything

The road doesn't care who's watching. Riding to demonstrate competence usually exposes its absence. If ego is involved, attention is already divided.

Don't "keep up"

Matching someone else's pace assumes their judgement matches yours. It rarely does. Riding well means riding at *your* edge, not someone else's.

Don't ride to escape something

Riding can regulate the mind, but it doesn't resolve what's being avoided. If I'm riding to dodge a conversation or decision, that avoidance will still be waiting when the helmet comes off.

Don't ignore discomfort

Discomfort demands attention whether you acknowledge it or not. Irritation becomes distraction, and distraction becomes error. If something feels off, it costs less to stop than to push through.

Don't assume familiarity equals safety

The roads I know best are where complacency appears first. Familiarity lowers vigilance without improving conditions. I ride my regular routes more conservatively than unfamiliar ones.

Don't confuse smoothness with slowness

Good riding often looks unremarkable. Smooth inputs aren't cautious—they're efficient. If a ride feels dramatic, something is probably being mishandled.

Don't override the early "no"

There's usually a moment before a bad ride where something feels wrong. Ignoring that signal is a choice. I try not to make it.

THINGS TO MAKE A HABIT OF...

Do maintain the bike before it asks

Mechanical failure is rarely sudden. Chains, tyres, and components complain long before they fail. Early attention preserves reliability—and attention.

Do treat tyres as mood stabilisers

Grip changes everything. Good tyres reduce hesitation, second-guessing, and tension. When tyres are right, riding becomes quieter—mentally and physically.

Do slow the pre-ride check when I'm distracted

If my head isn't settled, I don't rush the ritual. The check isn't just mechanical—it re-centres attention before movement begins.

Do keep the bike predictable

Smooth throttle, deliberate braking, and consistent inputs make the bike readable. Predictability isn't about control—it's about reducing surprise.

Do ride the conditions, not the plan

Plans assume cooperation from weather, traffic, and timing. Conditions rarely comply. I adjust without resentment and without trying to recover what was lost.

Do stop while the ride is still good

Ending a ride early often feels unsatisfying in the moment—and correct in hindsight. Restraint usually arrives before regret.

Do maintain my gear like it matters

If it touches me at speed, it deserves care. Clean visors reduce cognitive load. Comfortable gear keeps irritation from becoming distraction.

Do assume skill fades without attention

Competence isn't permanent. Confidence drifts without feedback. I assume I'm always a student—not out of doubt, but out of respect for risk.

Do notice patterns, not incidents

One bad ride is information. Repeated discomfort is instruction. I pay attention to trends rather than isolated mistakes.

Do ride with people who ride well

Judgement is contagious. So is recklessness. I choose riding partners the same way I choose mentors—quietly and deliberately.

Taken together, these habits aren't about riding perfectly or thinking correctly. They're about maintenance—the kind that keeps a man aligned rather than reactive. Jung wrote that what we refuse to face does not disappear; it returns as fate. Joseph Campbell understood that the hero's task is not escape, but return—changed, integrated, and more capable of carrying responsibility. Riding offers a small, honest arena where this work can't be outsourced. The bike reflects neglect quickly. So does the mind. Masculinity, when stripped of performance, looks less like bravado and more like stewardship: of attention, of judgement, of the systems that carry us forward. Maintenance isn't weakness. It's the quiet discipline that allows movement to continue without fracture—on the road, and everywhere else.

The reserve isn't there because you expect to fail—it's there because responsibility means preparing for the moments when you're human.

About the Author

Stephen Spiteri is a husband, father, motorcycle rider, and lifelong learner. He writes from lived experience rather than theory, exploring how motivation, discipline, and maintenance work together in modern life. His work reflects a belief that motivation initiates change, discipline sustains it, and maintenance preserves what matters over time. He values competence, responsibility, and attention as practical foundations for mental health and masculinity.